# CHURCH SIGNS ACROSS AMERICA

STEVE AND PAM PAULSON

THE OVERLOOK PRESS

WOODSTOCK & NEW YORK

# CHURCH SIGNS ACROSS AMERICA

PHOTOGRAPHS BY STEVE AND PAM PAULSON

THIS BOOK IS DEDICATED
TO THE MEMBERS OF
THESE CHURCHES WHO
SUPPORT THEIR SIGNS WITH
WORDS OF LOVE

"THE FRUIT OF THE SPIRIT IS LOVE..." GALATIANS 5:22

FIRST PUBLISHED IN THE UNITED STATES IN 2006 BY
THE OVERLOOK PRESS, PETER MAYER PUBLISHERS, INC.
WOODSTOCK & NEW YORK

WOODSTOCK:
ONE OVERLOOK DRIVE
WOODSTOCK, NY 12498
WWW.OVERLOOKPRESS.COM
[FOR INDIVIDUAL ORDERS, BULK AND SPECIAL SALES, CONTACT OUR WOODSTOCK OFFICE]

NEWYORK:
141 WOOSTER STREET
NEW YORK, NY 10012

CATALOGING-IN-PUBLICATION DATA IS AVAILABLE FROM THE LIBRARY OF CONGRESS

PHOTO EDITING BY PAM PAULSON AND FRED S. HIXON III.
MANUFACTURED IN CHINA
ISBN-10 1-58567-714-0 / ISBN-13 978-1-58567-714-6
3 5 7 9 8 6 4

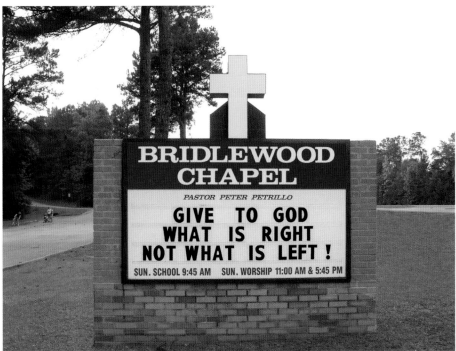

OZARK

ALABAMA

1

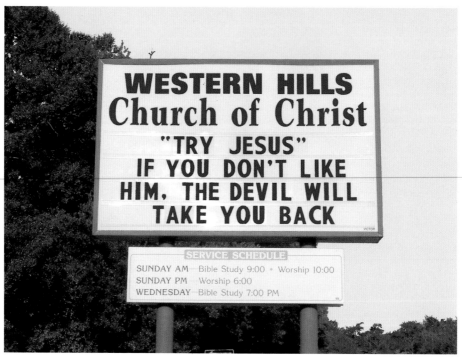

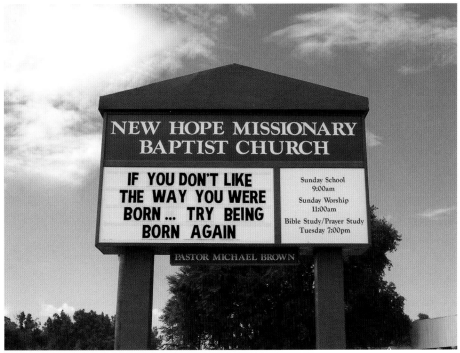

MOBILE

ALABAMA

ROBERTSDALE

ALABAMA

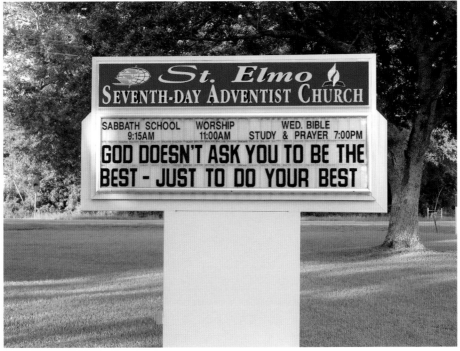

ST. ELMO

ALABAMA

CROSSROADS ASSEMBLY OF GOD
JIM SCHULZ PASTOR

NOTHING RUINS THE
TRUTH LIKE
STRECHING IT
SUN WORSHIP 1030 AM

ANCHORAGE

ALASKA

✝

WASILLA

ALASKA

PHOENIX
ARIZONA

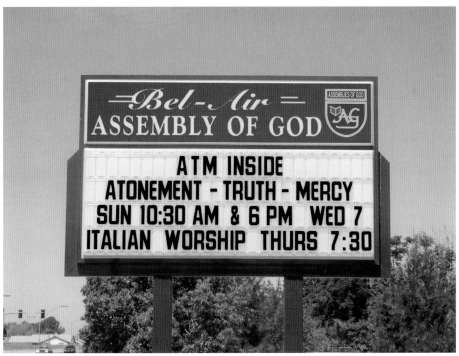

†

GLENDALE

ARIZONA

MOUNTAINBURG

ARKANSAS

NORTH LITTLE ROCK
ARKANSAS

LITTLE ROCK
ARKANSAS

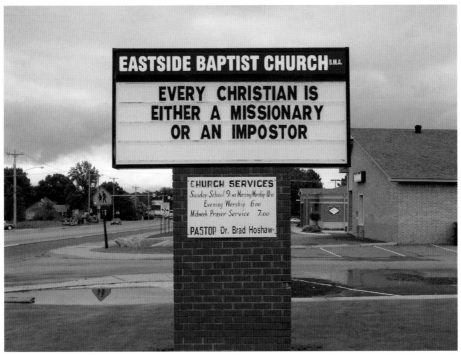

✝

CONWAY

ARKANSAS

† 

LOS ANGELES

CALIFORNIA

14

†

CANOGA PARK
CALIFORNIA

SIERRA MADRE
CALIFORNIA

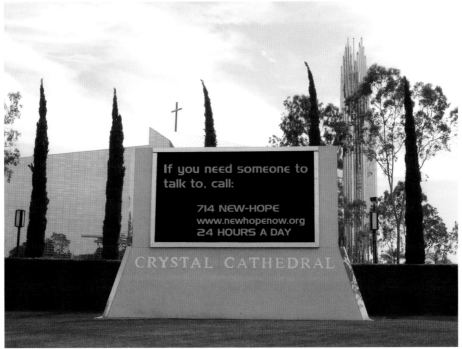

If you need someone to talk to, call:

714 NEW-HOPE
www.newhopenow.org
24 HOURS A DAY

CRYSTAL CATHEDRAL

†

GARDEN GROVE
CALIFORNIA

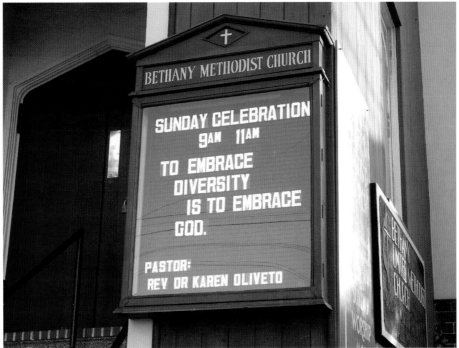

†

SAN FRANCISCO
CALIFORNIA

✝

ALTADENA
CALIFORNIA

SAN DIEGO

CALIFORNIA

REDONDO BEACH
CALIFORNIA

23

ARVADA

COLORADO

†

BURLINGTON
COLORADO

WORRY IS THE DARK ROOM
WHERE NEGATIVES DEVELOP

TRADITIONAL 8 AM - CONTEMP. & DEAF 10:30 AM

✝

DENVER
COLORADO

WHEAT RIDGE

COLORADO

†

NORWICH
CONNECTICUT

30

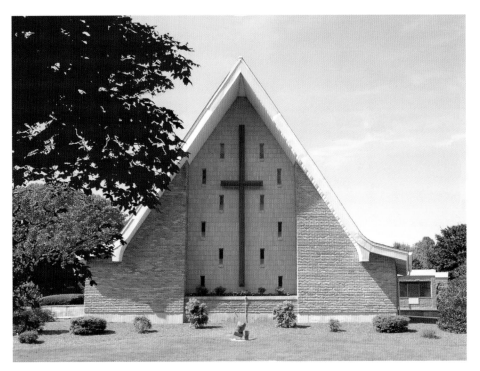

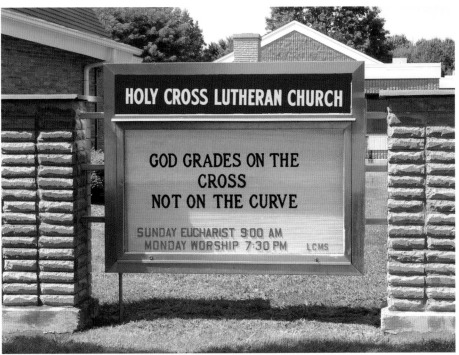

HOLY CROSS LUTHERAN CHURCH

GOD GRADES ON THE
CROSS
NOT ON THE CURVE

SUNDAY EUCHARIST 9:00 AM
MONDAY WORSHIP 7:30 PM    LCMS

TRUMBULL
CONNECTICUT

WILMINGTON

DELAWARE

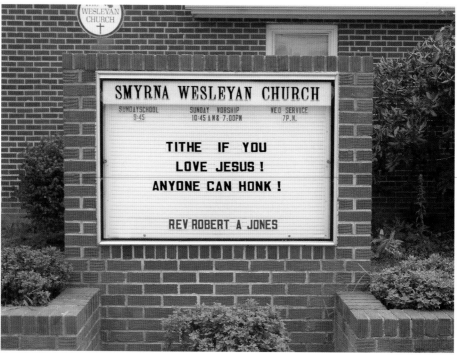

SMYRNA

DELAWARE

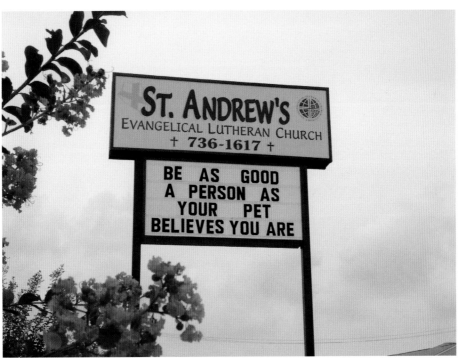

CAPE CORAL
FLORIDA

FORT OGDEN

FLORIDA

FORT MYERS
FLORIDA

✝

MOUNT DORA
FLORIDA

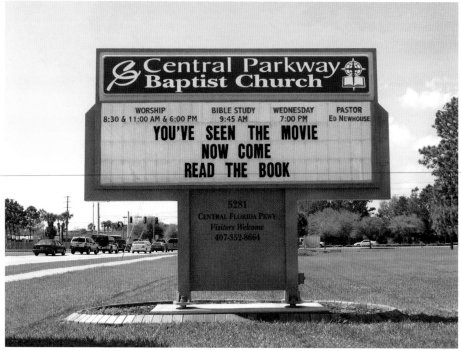

ORLANDO

FLORIDA

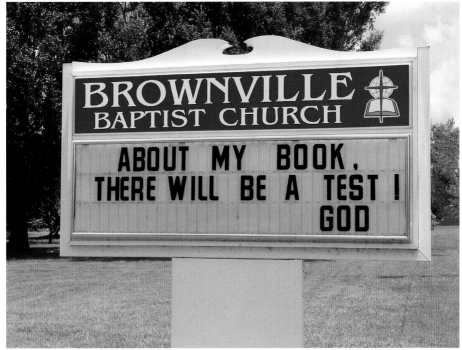

BROWNVILLE

FLORIDA

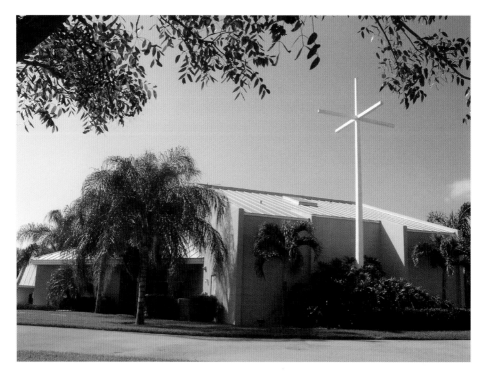

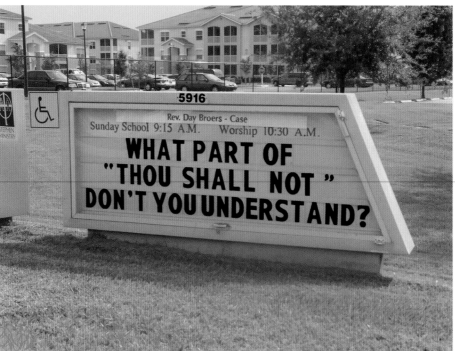

FORT MYERS

FLORIDA

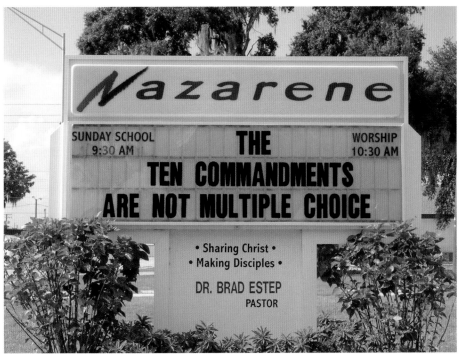

WINTER HAVEN
FLORIDA

43

ARCADIA

FLORIDA

44

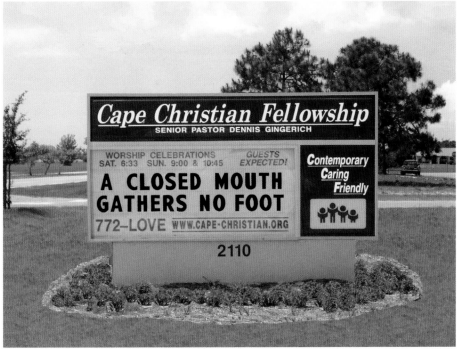

✝

CAPE CORAL

FLORIDA

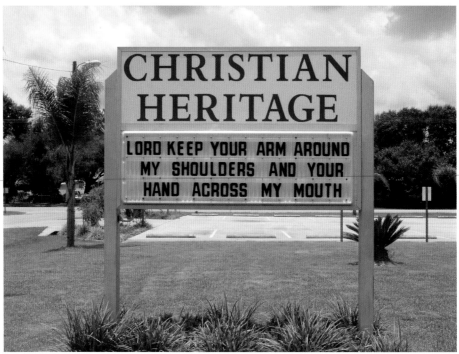

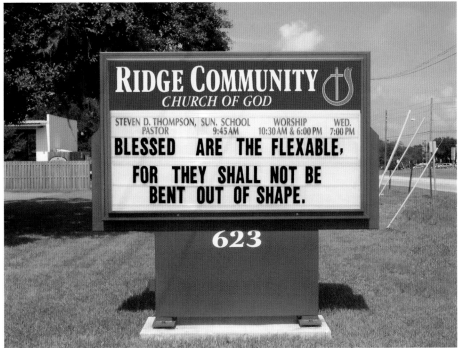

DUNDEE

FLORIDA

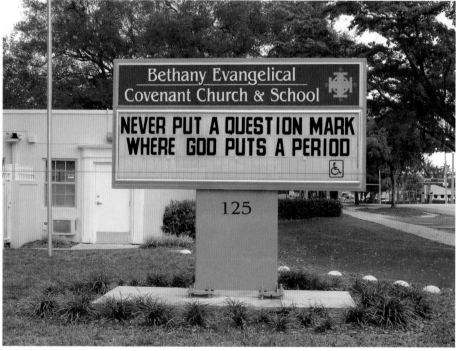

NORTH MIAMI
FLORIDA

FORT MYERS

FLORIDA

MARATHON

FLORIDA

VALDOSTA
GEORGIA

THOMASVILLE

GEORGIA

St. Augustine Road Church of Christ

THE BEST THING TO SPEND ON YOUR CHILDREN IS TIME

SUNDAY BIBLE CLASS : 10:00 AM   SUNDAY WORSHIP : 11:00 AM
EVENING WORSHIP : 6:00 PM   WED. BIBLE WORSHIP : 6:30 PM
MINISTER:  TOMMY SIMPSON

713

✝

VALDOSTA

GEORGIA

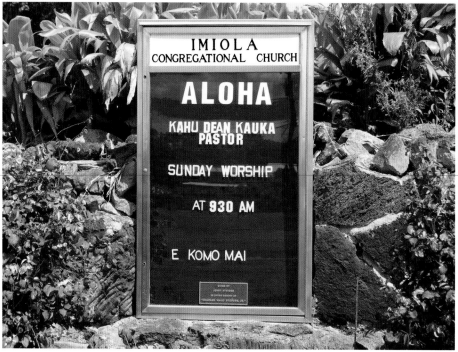

KAMUELA

HAWAII

†

HONOLULU
HAWAII

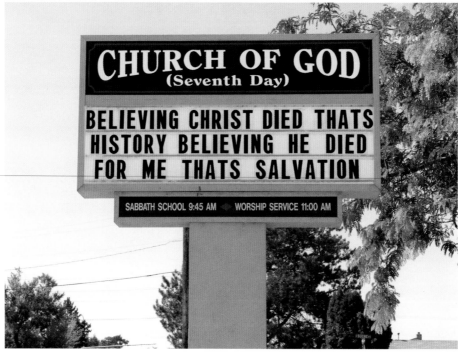

NAMPA

IDAHO

KIMBERLY

IDAHO

CHRIST THE KING

FORBIDDEN FRUIT
CREATES MANY JAMS
★WORSHIP★SUNDAY★9:00 AM★

†

NORMAL

ILLINOIS

JOLIET
ILLINOIS

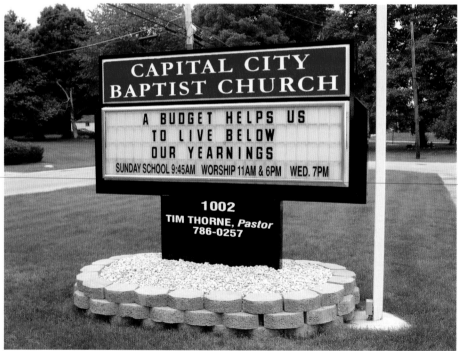

CAPITAL CITY
BAPTIST CHURCH

A BUDGET HELPS US
TO LIVE BELOW
OUR YEARNINGS

SUNDAY SCHOOL 9:45AM   WORSHIP 11AM & 6PM   WED. 7PM

1002
TIM THORNE, *Pastor*
786-0257

INDIANAPOLIS
INDIANA

SCOTTSBURG

INDIANA

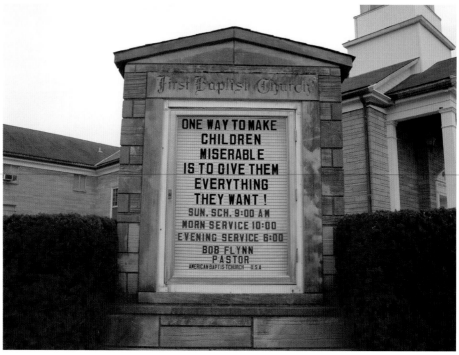

First Baptist Church

ONE WAY TO MAKE
CHILDREN
MISERABLE
IS TO GIVE THEM
EVERYTHING
THEY WANT !
SUN. SCH. 9:00 AM
MORN SERVICE 10:00
EVENING SERVICE 6:00
BOB FLYNN
PASTOR
AMERICAN BAPTIST CHURCH — U.S.A

SCOTTSBURG

INDIANA

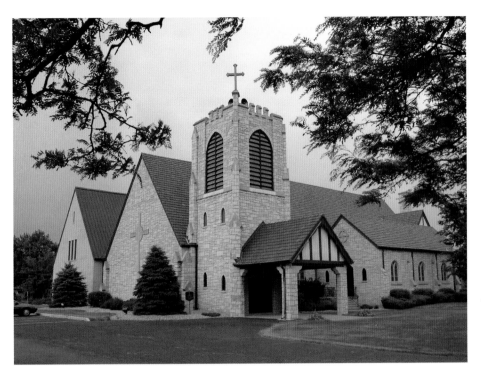

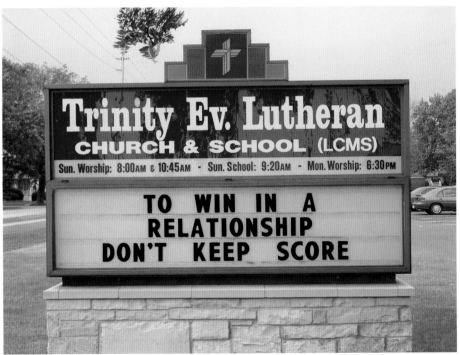

CROWN POINT
INDIANA

FIRST BAPTIST CHURCH

SINCE CHRIST DIED FOR US CAN WE DO LESS THAN LIVE FOR HIM

✝

CRAWFORDSVILLE

INDIANA

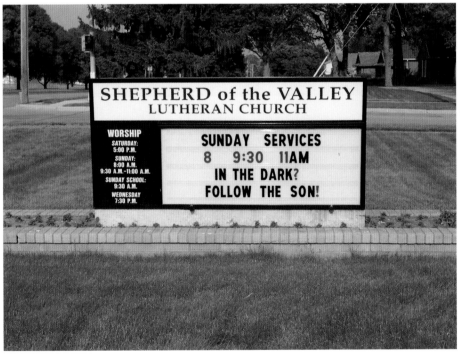

WEST DES MOINES
IOWA

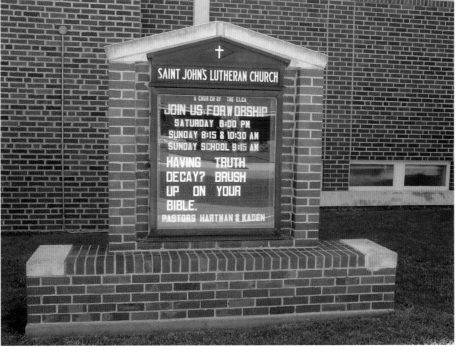

RUSSELL
KANSAS

✝

RUSSELL

KANSAS

TOPEKA

KANSAS

†

SHAWNEE

KANSAS

CORINTH

KENTUCKY

CHRISTIAN CHURCH

NO ONE GETS
INTO HEAVEN
WITHOUT A
RESERVATION
FOR MORE INFO
JOIN US SUNDAYS
AT 11

✝

HORSE CAVE
KENTUCKY

✝

ESTHERWOOD

LOUISIANA

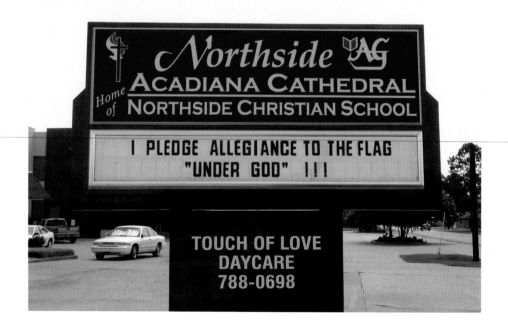

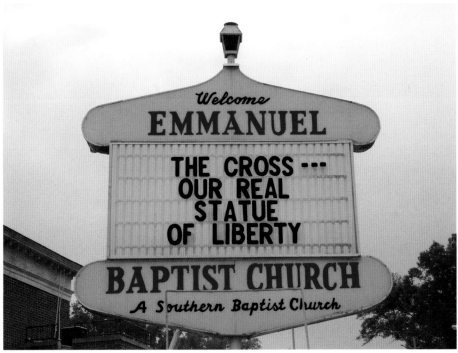

RUSTON
LOUISIANA

MONROE
LOUISIANA

CHALMETTE
LOUISIANA

FIRST
BAPTIST CHURCH
SANFORD, MAINE

AMERICAN BAPTIST CHURCH
REV. VIRGINIA E. GASS

THE MESSAGE
OF CHRIST
IS HOPE

9:30 MORNING WORSHIP
ALL ARE WELCOME

†

SANFORD
MAINE

AUBURN
MAINE

BEL AIR

MARYLAND

ABERDEEN

MARYLAND

LAWRENCE
MASSACHUSETTS

ATTLEBORO
MASSACHUSETTS

SAINT JOSEPH
MICHIGAN

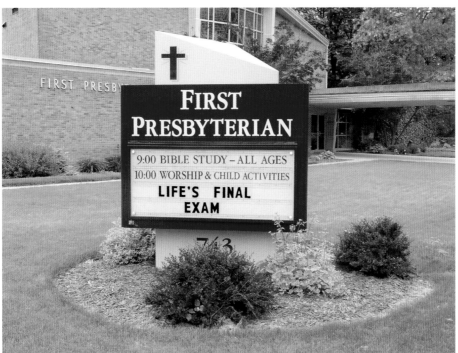

JACKSON
MICHIGAN

MAIN STREET UNITED
METHODIST CHURCH
BAY ST LOUIS MS

WHEN THE LAST
TRUMPET SOUNDS
WE'RE OUTTA HERE

WORSHIP 9 & 11

✝

BAY SAINT LOUIS
MISSISSIPPI

HICKMAN MILLS
Community Christian Church
LIFE'S OBSTACLES
AHEAD - NEED A
GUIDE ?

BRIDGETON
MISSOURI

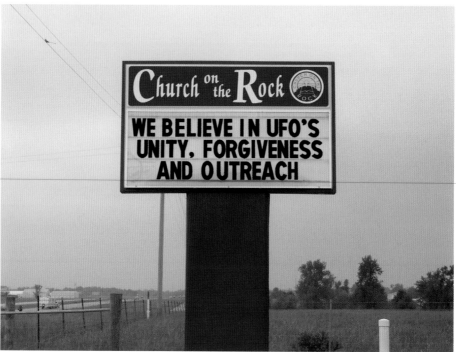

HARRISONVILLE
MISSOURI

✝

HELENA

MONTANA

NORTH PLATTE
NEBRASKA

LEXINGTON
NEBRASKA

GATES OF PRAISE

FOR A HEALTHY HEART
EXERCISE YOUR FAITH

740

†

LINCOLN
NEBRASKA

†

LAS VEGAS
NEVADA

PLEASANT STREET UNITED METHODIST CHURCH
REV JIM LUNDIN
SUNDAY WORSHIP
9:00AM
GOD IS NOT
FINISED WITH US

†

SALEM
NEW HAMPSHIRE

†

CLAREMONT
NEW HAMPSHIRE

†

PORTSMOUTH
NEW HAMPSHIRE

STEWARTSVILLE

NEW JERSEY

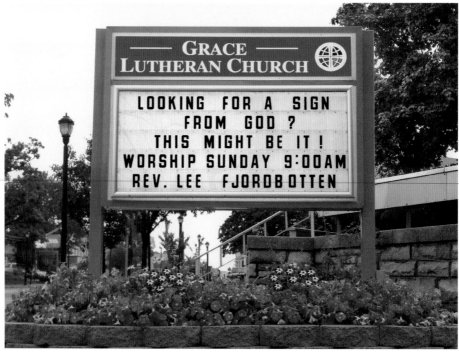

GRACE
LUTHERAN CHURCH

LOOKING FOR A SIGN
FROM GOD ?
THIS MIGHT BE IT !
WORSHIP SUNDAY 9:00AM
REV. LEE FJORDBOTTEN

✝

NORTH ARLINGTON
NEW JERSEY

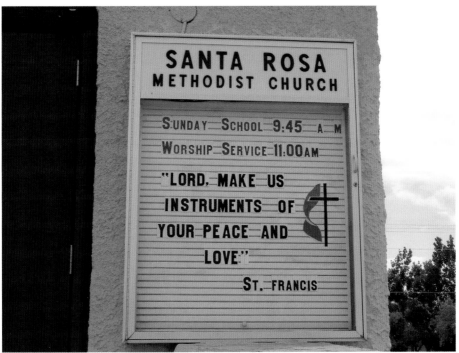

SANTA ROSA
NEW MEXICO

DELMAR

NEW YORK

†

STATESVILLE
NORTH CAROLINA

†

DAYTON
OHIO

116

FAIRFIELD
OHIO

FRANKLIN
OHIO

FAIRFIELD

OHIO

NEW PARIS
OHIO

GRATIS

OHIO

KETTERING

OHIO

†

OKLAHOMA CITY

OKLAHOMA

✝

LONE GROVE
OKLAHOMA

PHILADELPHIA

PENNSYLVANIA

✝

HELLERTOWN

PENNSYLVANIA

PHILADELPHIA

PENNSYLVANIA

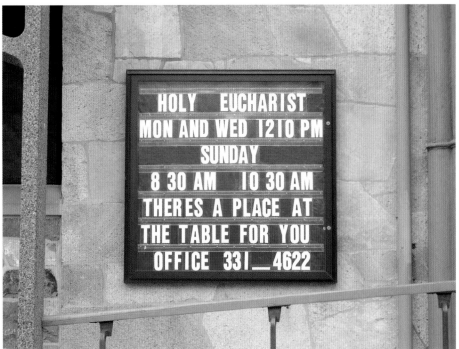

WARRENVILLE

SOUTH CAROLINA

WINDSOR

SOUTH CAROLINA

SIOUX FALLS
SOUTH DAKOTA

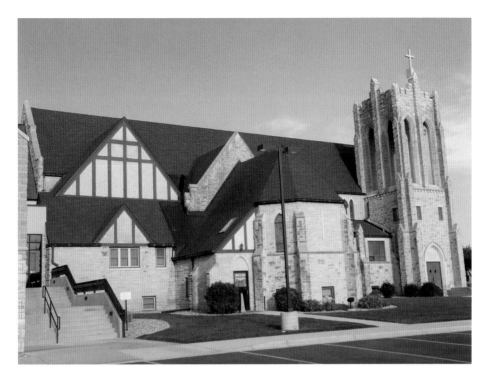

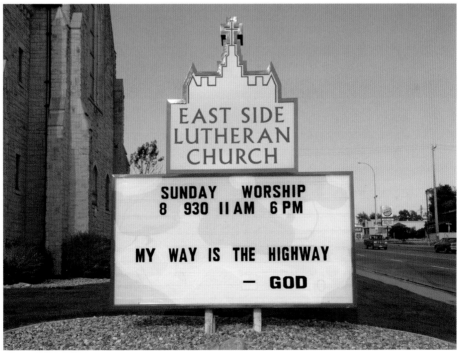

✝

SIOUX FALLS
SOUTH DAKOTA

135

FELLOWSHIP CHURCH
FREE WILL BAPTIST

SUNDAY SCHOOL 9:00AM    WORSHIP 10:00AM & 6:00PM    WED. 7:00PM

WHEN ALL IS SAID AND DONE THERE IS MORE SAID THAN DONE

†

ANTIOCH

TENNESSEE

NASHVILLE
TENNESSEE

138

KNOXVILLE

TENNESSEE

NASHVILLE
TENNESSEE

140

✝

AMARILLO
TEXAS

✝

BEAUMONT

TEXAS

142

BEAUMONT

TEXAS

144

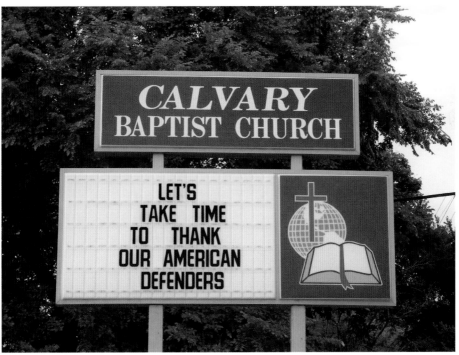

CALVARY BAPTIST CHURCH

DO NOT LET THE GOOD
THINGS IN LIFE ROB
YOU OF THE BEST

SUNDAY WORSHIP 9:30

✝

SPRINGFIELD
VERMONT

147

IMMANUEL EPISCOPAL CHURCH

JOIN US FOR WORSHIP
Eucharist & Sunday School
SUNDAY - 9:30am
EVENING PRAYER
MONDAY - 4:00pm
Eucharist with Healing
WEDNESDAY - 12:15pm

COMMUNITY EVENTS
SUNDAY - A.A. - 8:00pm
COMMUNITY SUPPER
MONDAY - 5:00pm
T.O.P.S.
TUESDAY - 7:00pm
ALANON
WEDNESDAY - 8:00pm

GOD TRULY LOVES
▶ YOU ◀
WOW !

BELLOWS FALLS
VERMONT

THE TONGUE WEIGHS ALMOST NOTHING BUT FEW CAN HOLD IT

WORSHIP – 9:45    SUNDAY SCHOOL – 10.45
REV. BOB CARBARY    276-686-4422

✝

WYTHEVILLE

VIRGINIA

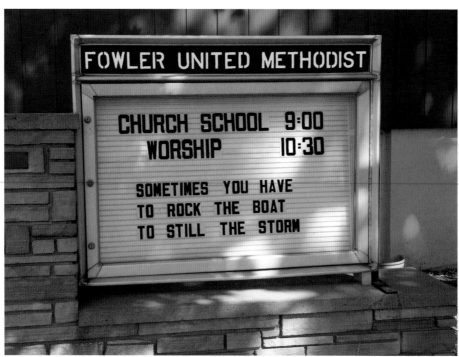

✝

SPOKANE
WASHINGTON

†

PASCO
WASHINGTON

151

PASCO
WASHINGTON

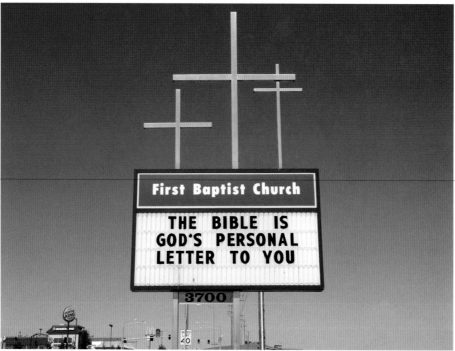

KENNEWICK
WASHINGTON

✝

KENNEWICK
WASHINGTON

PRINCETON
WEST VIRGINIA

PRINCETON
WEST VIRGINIA

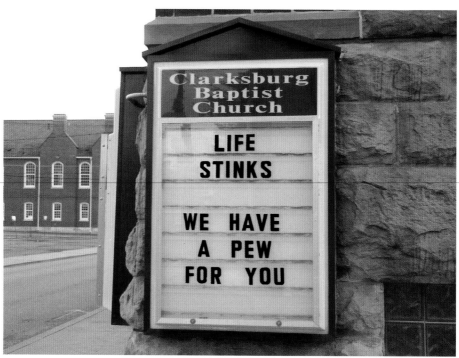

CLARKSBURG
WEST VIRGINIA

Maranatha
Baptist Church
& CHRISTIAN ACADEMY

AS WE HAVE
OPPORTUNITY LET US
DO GOOD UNTO ALL
MEN
GALATIANS 6 10

†

PRINCETON
WEST VIRGINIA

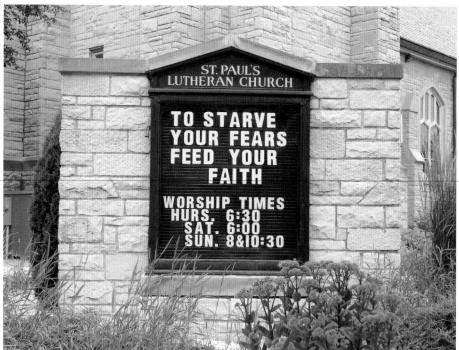

ST. PAUL'S
LUTHERAN CHURCH

TO STARVE
YOUR FEARS
FEED YOUR
FAITH

WORSHIP TIMES
HURS. 6:30
SAT. 6:00
SUN. 8&10:30

✝

JANESVILLE
WISCONSIN

A HEART THAT LOVES
IS ALWAYS YOUNG.
GREEK PROVERB

✝

LA CROSSE
WISCONSIN